CREATE YOUR
BEST HOLIDAYS

Tips to Easily Handle
Holiday Stresses and
Have Fun!

Pat Brill

TABLE OF CONTENTS

Copyright

An Important Note

I hope this guide; *Create Your Best Holiday* helps you minimize stress and build enjoyment throughout the holiday season. The information provided in this guide is based on my research, as well as my life knowledge around the subject. I used to have a holiday "Open House" every Christmas Eve and over the years have created a plan that allows me to enjoy the holidays.

I can't guarantee you will not feel stress.
Take the knowledge and tools offered in
this guide and create a plan that ensures
that you have your best holidays.

Introduction

Every single person has experienced individual events that cause them stress. No one is immune to this intense feeling. When the holiday season comes around, it seems that we automatically think it's going to be stressful. Mainly because in the past it may have been your total responsibility and that's stressful. I believe it's a habit to be stressed during the holidays and you can create enjoyable, relaxing and fun holidays.

If in the past, or now, you have felt any of the following, it's probably safe to say that you are already dealing with some form of stress:

* You are overly cranky

* You find it difficult to get a good night's rest

* You are on a weight roller coaster

* You find yourself more "on edge"

* You feel you can never get anything done

* Or fill in the blank around what you feel with holiday stress.

You can this year decide to create your best holiday without adding lots of stress.

That is why I created this guide to provide you with the tools to create the holiday that brings you and your love one's pleasure.

Included here will be some things you can do to boost your energy and relieve stress throughout the holiday gatherings, shopping sprees, and other unplanned surprises that may come your way!

Importance of Holidays

Holidays are important as they are celebrated with families, friends, neighborhoods and throughout the world.

Each person has their own experiences, wishes, and images around the holidays.

Memories are captured over each year, and this continuity creates within us a belief around how we should celebrate the holidays.

You can change your vision of the holidays and create time together that brings enjoyment for all.

The traditional year-end holidays are called Festivals of Light or Winter Solstice holidays which include Christmas, Diwali, Hanukkah, Kwanzaa, Saint Lucy's Day, Lunar New Year and Zoroastrian Solstice Celebration.

There are many more celebrations that occur throughout the year, though the

Festivals of Light brings the major traditional holidays.

Most people have experience one of the traditional holidays. These ritual celebrations give people time to stop what they are doing, relax, connect with others and create new memories together. Sometimes the memories aren't great, though we always seem to want to come together and find that special place to celebrate the holiday.

Holidays serve a purpose either to celebrate a religious or government event and bring people together for the occasion.

In a perfect world, holidays are great opportunities to bring the family together and build stronger relationships with everyone. However, you decide how to celebrate your holiday, and how you can create your best holiday. Creating the best holiday does not mean elaborate, fancy, expensive, but rather a holiday that brings people together to celebrate the occasion and each other.

How do you want to bring people together for the holidays?

Take the time to plan what works best for you, get the help you need and keep within a budget that doesn't stress you out the rest of the year. This guide will provide you with ways to create a comfortable gathering with others in your life.

Holidays are not about "things," instead they are experiences shared together. So, let's see how you can create the best holiday for you.

STRESS-REDUCING TIPS

Stick to a Normal Schedule

It's important for **all** family members, not just you, to stick to a regular schedule. Everyone needs to have a routine, especially children. We thrive on it. Also, children depend on it! Changing regular routines can add unnecessary stress to you and your family. So, try to keep up with your set schedules of eating, sleeping, TV time, and of course play times.

With the emotional excitement of the holidays, friends and family members coming for unannounced visits, and social "get-togethers," it can be a bit more difficult to stick to your normal daily routines. It is possible if you have a solid support system (i.e., a spouse, close family member, or a valued friend that are willing to help you "stick with it").

You can choose to have an enjoyable holiday season.

You can always make small adjustments to your routine to fit that day's schedule of "hectic" events and be able to keep to your schedule.

Express Your Feelings

Let others know how you feel by sharing it with them in a positive way. Find the time to let them know how much you love them. Sharing a message of love helps relieve your stress as well as their stress.

Holidays can bring about irritation between two people or within a family. If things are bothering you, share it. Though do it in a manner that doesn't put more stress on yourself or the other person!

Having a family "chat session" about what everyone is feeling can not only strengthen the bonds between everyone but also alleviate some of the normal stresses associated with the holidays.

Ensure that this particular time isn't a "gripe session." Don't let your stressful feelings turn into anger and expressed at the expense of another person's feelings.

Channel your energetic feelings in more productive ways than being hurtful.

Discuss what you are feeling and use "I" statements to express your feelings. For example, "I feel overwhelmed by all there needs to be done for the holidays." If you say "You are not doing anything" it will create more tension between yourself and others.

Be open for constructive ways that each of you can work together to solve any tensions or problems. Take positive steps towards expressing yourself and understanding the feelings of others.

Ask for Help

It's not as devastating as you might think. It's quite easy! If you are having a tough time shouldering all the responsibilities that are upon you, ask someone to help you with them.

You could do this by dividing up different tasks that are on your holiday list of things to get done. Of course, you'll want to be sure that whatever work you assign to a family member is "age appropriate." Meaning you don't want to give your ten year old the job of hanging outdoor lights on the roof! So, make sure that you delegate these responsibilities as they fit the laborer.

Create a fun "To Do" list with everyone's

name next to the task, with a surprise to be shared by all when the work is done. Celebrate when done and create a pre-holiday family gathering -- a special night just for all the hard workers.

Sometimes holiday time brings out "sadness" and other distressing emotions. If your need for help is more of an emotional nature, speak with someone you trust about what you are feeling. We put a lot of stress upon ourselves when we demand that we be "happy" during the holiday season. Find ways to take care of yourself during this time of the year.

Know Your Limits and Follow Them

Be careful not to add too much on your

"to do" list. Ensure that your "to do" list is realistic in what can get done during the holidays, but also what you can afford to spend. Don't over-extend yourself or your finances. Remember, the thing that people will remember most is that you were there with them, sharing precious time to celebrate the joy of being together and not the physical gifts they received.

You are worth more than a little "gift." And that is what will create lasting memories for everyone! And, don't be too harsh on yourself for not getting that expensive video game or a collectible doll for the children. Do what you can and nothing more. Don't place high expectations on yourself, and don't make promises you simply cannot keep. Limiting what you can realistically will help reduce the stresses you put on yourself.

Don't Strive for "Perfection"

Nobody's perfect. Nothing can be perfect, so don't expect that! Do what you can and be happy knowing that you did all you could to make it a wonderful holiday. Trying to create a "picture perfect" holiday gathering can add unnecessary stress to your life and others around you. Not everyone gets along, people don't like the gift your purchased, and there isn't enough time or money to make it perfect.

Make a promise to yourself that you will only do what you can without placing too much pressure on yourself to get it all done.

Put more of the emphasis on enjoying the people in your life.

During the holiday season, we do tend to expect others to behave in a specific manner. A good thing to keep in mind is that you have no control over anyone other than yourself. They will do what they do, and that's the end of it!
There will be members of your family that help out readily, others that prefer to sit down. Maybe you have a member of your family that is not happy around

holidays…do not try to change him or her.

Instead, try not to let the actions of others within your circle of family or friends discourage you from having a great holiday season. People will be who they are, and you should learn to let go of any personal expectations of how you want the holiday gatherings to be. Do you need to add more stress to your life? No, so make sure you are creating a holiday season that you enjoy.

Types of Families That Celebrate the Holidays?

Families are not all traditional Mother and Father living in the same household…there are a lot of divorced, step family combinations, and same gender adults that are considered families. Then add to the family mix the in-laws. So how do you solve the problem of the various family units?   Here are some ideas to help you handle this challenging situation:

- Celebrate Christmas on the 24th, 25th and 26th.   You can cover the divorced and in-law family combinations on each day.   Then rotate each year.

- If you celebrate another holiday during the Winter season, then use the days before and after to have time with all the essential people in your life.

- If it is just the in-laws, each year switch holidays each year between families.

- The most important decision is to make your own decision. Don't get involved with everyone's hurt feelings. Instead, explain the situation, and your solution to the problem and stick with it.

- Communicate early in the holiday season so this way for the actual holiday everyone can digest your decision and are hopefully ready to celebrate the season.

- Try to get a consensus around what the holidays entail, so everyone is on board, though if you can't, you may need to decide.

- Keep your vision of a simple, caring and relaxing holiday together and share it with others.

What Makes the Holiday Season Special for You?

Are the holidays a time of sharing and togetherness? Is it a time of sadness, loss or grief over past experiences? What makes the holidays special may be different for each family member or friend depending on events that have occurred in their lives.

If something pleasant has occurred for someone, that's what they will tend to remember about the holiday seasons. If the person has experienced an incredible loss, then more than likely they will not be in a very celebratory mood. Don't let this discourage you from having a happy holiday though.

Expectations take a lot of energy and if they are not met…disappointment. If you intend to have a happy celebration, share it and let each person decide how much of it they want to take. Create your magic and enjoy it.

When I was growing up, I remembered the holidays were filled with magic. We didn't have a lot of money, but Christmas was a special time, where we got at least one special toy we wanted, along with needed clothes.   The adults created the magic.

Then I grew up and had a child of my own. My partner didn't grow up with the magic I felt as a child, so didn't understand what I meant.   My son had just turned two and that Christmas I made a conscious decision to create my magic. There was no magic wand; instead, I changed my thoughts about my expectations that my partner is active in creating the magic.   I didn't need him to create the magic, though he could come along for the ride, and I was going to have fun and create that special magic for my son.

My energy changed around the holidays because I choose to enjoy the time…and I did. I also have a better relationship with my partner.

Going Home to the Family

We all have images, hopes, and expectations around the holidays and especially with our families. No family is perfect so how can you create the best holiday for yourself? Here are some ideas:

- Probably not a good idea to discuss those highly sensitive subjects, unless your family has a great sense of humor. Different generations may have different political allegiances…unless you can have a healthy family discussion, I wouldn't engage in it.

- Keep the season in mind...what is essential ...sharing and giving love to the people that are important in your life.

- If there is a person in the family that irritates you, try to go out of your way to be caring, or stay away from them. They are not going to change, so why spoil your holidays because of their personality.

- If someone gets under your skin, as family members sometimes can do, take a deep breath, excuse yourself and go out for a breath of fresh air.

If fresh air isn't your thing, help the host out. If you are the host, then find something that needs to be done.

- Leave your expectations at the door and bring your good will to everyone there. Expectations irritate you. Bring your desire to enjoy the people in your family.
- Tap into your sense of humor, have fun and enjoy yourself.

Do Some Realistic Planning

Never underestimate the value of a good plan! Your plan needs to be one that is within your ability to complete. Try not to set too many goals for yourself that you couldn't possibly get done in each day. Planning allows you to space out the many tasks of the holiday season.

Every year, many people wait until the very last minute to get everything done all at once. Not a good idea. What happens? You know you have a big shopping list to take care of, so you dash out the door quick as you can, get into the car, speed off into the night to get it all finished up before the stores close. Guess what? There are probably a hundred other people doing the same thing you are at that very moment!

Now, not only do you have to deal with trying to get those things on your shopping list, you're going to have to make your way through the heavy traffic, crowded stores, and lengthy check out waits. What if you spend all that time searching for a highly sought-after item only to find out that they are entirely out of stock! Now you must try your luck at a different store altogether.

You can avoid all this stress by creating a plan. Even if you only have one month left to finish your shopping, you could take an extra hour out of each day to pick up those items on your list before the mad holiday buying rush.

The best way to have a good, "less stress" holiday plan is to start planning soon after the holiday. You can get great bargains through "after holiday" sales and take those items, cross them off your list, and put them up for safe-keeping until next year's holiday. Also, there's no rush to complete the tasks on your "to do" list since you have an entire year to get them done! *Remember this for January 1ˢᵗ.*

I rarely step into a store anymore as I do most of my shopping online. Black Friday is for the adventuresome people who are tactile and need to see and touch. I'm a Cyber Monday person, and I usually do an excellent job in finding the right present for the people on my list. I should tell you I cut my list down to mainly the children in the family. I know that others can't be that limited in their list, though there are creative ideas further on in this guide that you could potentially use to change your shopping habits.

At the end of this guide, I've added different planning sheets to make your life easier.

Take A Break!

With everything that's going on during the holiday season, it's essential to make some time to relax. Whether it's stopping at the corner Cafe for a cup of coffee, treating yourself to a non-holiday themed movie, or setting down to a peaceful bite to eat, doing just one small thing to take yourself away from the list of "To Do" of the holiday season and make an enjoyable mental sigh of relief!

You can take a mini-break by using some basic relaxation breathing techniques that can aid you in releasing stress. Stop whatever it is you're doing, close your eyes, and take in a five deep, cleansing, breaths. Breathe in and breathe out slowly. You will find this to be very soothing in times of high stress. As the body takes in more oxygen, it reduces the number of hormonal stress releases within the body. Thereby, reducing the physical feelings of stress.

If you have time in your busy day, go home and take a short, restful nap. Short naps, or catnaps, can help to "recharge" your mental batteries.

You could even end your day with a sweet-smelling, muscle relaxing, steamy bath. Light some candles, shut out the world, and retreat to the most private room in your home! Don't have time for a bath? Then how about a nice, hot, cup of chamomile tea?

Use whatever common stress-busters that work best for you. Just make sure you set aside some time to do them over the course of the holidays.

Be Budget Conscious

A common occurrence with many people during the holidays is the problem of overspending. Of course, everyone wants to make those they care for as happy as possible by getting them their every whim. But this isn't realistic. Especially with the rising costs that surround our life. (See the Holiday Budget List at the end of the guide.)

If you haven't set a clear-cut budget for your holiday spending, DO IT! Not only that, but you *must stick with it*. Spending more than what you have is easy to do. Those that have an extensive line of credit, it becomes easier to go over budget.

An important fact to keep in your mind is that just because the money is available to you doesn't mean you have to spend it. Even Santa makes a list and checks it twice :-) You should do the same.

If you have a big list of gifts, why not try using the "hat trick" or "Secret Santa!" Write down each person's name on a small scrap of paper and put it in a hat. Have each family member then select one of the paper scraps. The name they choose is the only person they need to buy a gift. This hat exercise will spread the shopping responsibility throughout the family and reduce the amount of stress on you.

Half of my family celebrate Christmas, and the other half celebrate Hanukkah.

The Open House on Christmas Eve celebrates Christmas. I used to bring the Jewish side of the family together for a "Secret Santa," until my creative nephew called it a "Hanukkah Hush Hush." There we get one name, bought one present, and we all open our presents at the gathering. This way the spirit of gift giving is still there without having to spend lots of money to enjoy giving to others.

If you are not all together, have one person create a master list and match up names, emailing or calling the people with the name they need to buy a present. A perfect way to handle the adults in the family. You may want to include the children, though families are reluctant to add them with only one gift. You can decide what works best for your family.

Don't Be Afraid to Say No

It's hard to tell someone "no," isn't it? And that's completely understandable. No one wants to look into the hopeful eyes of someone you care for and say this word. Or to be looked upon as the "bad guy." You may feel as if you are letting them down, or making them unhappy by saying no. There are times you must do just that. Otherwise, you could create more stress for yourself:

- by having an added responsibility to provide that person with whatever it is they asked of you, or

- by trying to attain it and being
  unsuccessful, or

- spending too much money

By using this one word "no," you can save yourself tons of unwanted stress during the holiday season.

Practice "Giving"

The true spirit of the holiday season is about the gift of giving. That doesn't mean to run out and grab some last-minute charity presents for the local homeless shelter (although that is a beautiful thing to do). What I'm referring to here is to donate some *time* to help a local charity. Many times, this precious gift is more important than that of a monetary hand. However, if all you can offer is a donation of gifts or money, then give it!

You will be surprised at how fantastic you feel inside after doing so. Now, if you absolutely cannot do any of those things, why not help a neighbor. Your neighbor would appreciate an extra hand in something they are not good at…and you are!

After shopping, don't just smile and wish a happy holiday to that "bell-ringer" standing outside in the cold hoping for a few pennies to help their organization. Give them your change from your purchase you just made inside. If you already do this, keep doing it! You know firsthand how quickly it brings a joyous smile to your face from the inside out.

Be sure to get your children involved if you have them. Instilling the spirit of giving will carry something special within them for a lifetime.

Take Your Time

Often, people are always in a rush. Having an internal time clock can cause you excessive amounts of stress. Why are you pushing yourself? It will still take you the same amount of time to do whatever you need to get done. So, take the time to slow down.

Enjoy your time outside. So, there's a heap of traffic? So, what! If you don't like all the traffic, then try and structure your schedule around a time when there's less of it. Take a weekday off from work and do some of your more shopping in the morning. You'll get done faster, and you'll have more time to relax in the evening before you head back to work the next day.

If it's impossible for you to do that, then try shopping later. Sure, you might miss out on a couple of hours of extra sleep, but you'll have that much more accomplished and can make up for the lost rest on the weekend.

Slow yourself down and take more time to get things done. That means making more time available for such tasks.

The reason for slowing down is that you can enjoy what you are doing. You may find yourself deciding not to do some things that are not so important.

We look forward to the experience of being happy on that special holiday, never realizing that it is not just the actual day that makes the holiday special…it's all the time up to that holiday. Set the mood for all that you do and create your happiness doing each task. For example:

- When you are buying a gift for someone in your life, enjoy thinking about them. What do they like, what would make them happy?

- Sending out holiday cards -- either eliminate that task from your holiday list of "to do's" or make it a family party. If it's up to you to complete this task, and it's important to you, then make yourself a great dinner, and after, while drinking your tea or coffee, you can fill out the cards.

- When you are baking a holiday cookie or cake recipe, invite others to join you, or make a pot of tea and sip it while you are making your recipe.

- Have a "cookie" party where everyone makes a big bunch of only one of their favorite holiday cookies. They bring their big bunch of one cookie recipe to your house and everyone exchanges cookies. This way each of you now has a variety of holiday cookie selections. You will have to do a little planning here to make sure everyone doesn't bring the same chocolate chip cookie. Also, they need to bring their containers to take home their stash.

- Wrapping presents…put on some great music to give you energy and relaxation.

- Take any task that you put on your "to do" list and figure out a way to make it fun and relaxing. When that special day finally arrives, you would have accumulated so many fantastic fun and exciting experiences.

Take Care of YOU

To reduce even more stress, try picking up a little something for yourself. Or treat yourself to a relaxing manicure, facial, or massage. Taking care of yourself can do wonders for reducing holiday stress levels. Those aren't the only things you can do though. Take a walk in the park, drive the long route home after a busy day of shopping or working, and treat yourself to ice cream! Find time to do something you can do with yourself and by yourself.

Use Those "Time-Savers" Along the Way

Paper plates, disposable silverware, plastic cups, one-use aluminum baking pans, and napkins can cut down on your workload when throwing a friendly get-together. No one likes cleaning up after a party, especially a person that must do most of the work! If you are not comfortable in using plastic or disposable products, then this time saver will not work for you. You will need to include clean up on your "to do" list, though there are usually helpers to gather to make the job easier and time to talk together.

If you still have a few extra weeks before presents need wrapping, why not shop online and from the comfort of your home. Many internet shops even include gift-wrapping before the package is sent out for a small fee. So why not give it a try? A great way to send gifts to friends or family across the country, or world for that matter.

If you want to send gifts to a person in

another country, purchase that gift on Amazon website in that country.

Online resources are great for the very busy person who doesn't want to stand in line. You can sip a cup of tea or coffee while you open the box of gifts just delivered to your home.

Say "Thank You"

Everyone enjoys receiving the gift of a well-deserved "thank you." Your friends and family like to know that you truly appreciated the time and effort it took them to select your gift, so take some time and send them a lovely Thank You card, including a personal comment and not just your signature.

In the age of technology, we send emails to thank others for their kindness. Some people don't want to add more paper to the world, so sign up for e-cards and send a lovely note thanking the person for the gift. Decide which way you want to thank a person and don't forget to do it. Anyone who helps you through the holiday season, make sure you thank them. It can be the cashier who just packed up your groceries, or to the person who wrapped the gift for you. A simple "thank you" goes a long way to adding goodwill to all people.

I know you are busy and it is just one more thing to do…but make a game out of it. See how many people smile or how many times you can say "thank you" during your day. You will slow down and enjoy the season with this one act.

Leave Yourself Extra Time for the Unexpected

Delays are a part of everyday living but seem to heighten around the holiday hustle and bustle. There are lots of people traveling, shopping, and busy with festive activities, so be sure you give yourself enough time to account for these delays in getting where you're going.

In addition to this, winter weather can be, often be unpredictable, which can lead to back-ups in street traffic, delayed or even canceled flights, and other scheduled transportation systems.

Psych yourself up for this ahead of time so that you might handle the stress a little better. Bring some reading, letter writing or other "to do" activities with you so you can make waiting time more manageable for you.   If you are in the car, put in your glove compartment music that helps you relax.   Another great tool to use while waiting is listening to books on tape or your iPhone.

Something else you could do as far as getting to appointments on time is to set your clocks a half hour faster. Fool yourself into thinking that it is later than it is. Then you'll be happily surprised when you end up at your destination on time, or even early!

There are practically dozens and dozens of ways to fight holiday stress. *Why not create your own "stress buster" which you can enjoy and share with others?*

RESOURCES

Shopping Tips

Safety

- If you are out late shopping, ask the security guard at the shopping center to walk you to your car.
- Shop in groups
- Be careful with your cash and credit cards

Other Ideas

- If there is a gift that several people on your list would like, then buy duplicates. Maybe there is a slight variation in the item so that it can be different. However, if a couple

of people on your list like to shop at a specific store…gift certificates always work just fine.

- Ask the people to give you several gift ideas and they still won't know what you will be giving them.

- If you have a large item to wrap, an inexpensive way to do this is to buy a paper holiday tablecloth and use it to wrap that extra-large gift.

- Create a central location in your house to put presents, wrapping paper, etc.

Shipping

- Have the Post Office come to you and pick up those packages. Check out <u>USPS</u> and see if they work for you.

- Ship early because the lines get so long at the last moment. Time is important during a busy holiday season, so don't wait on line.

- If you are sending gifts out of the country, shipping early is a must if you want the gift to arrive on time. Or don't worry and buy online and let them ship it for you. Buy at a store that is in the country, so your shipping costs are less.

Food

- Keep some extra nibbles in the freezer for the spontaneous get together.

- Make extra dinners and put into the freezer…just in case. If not, you have a completed dinner for the family.

- Have some cider handy, add some nutmeg and cinnamon, simmer on the stove, and you will be right in the holiday spirit. The smell alone makes the home warm and comfortable, and the taste is excellent.

- Keep a bottle or two of wine available on the shelf and this way you are ready to celebrate with an unexpected guest.

BUDGET

How Much Can You Spend?

- Review how much money you
  want to spend on everything during
  the holidays.

- How much you will spend on gifts

- How much for holiday party or
  special dinners – food and drinks

- Don't forget all the little extras:
  invites, wrapping paper, holiday
  cards, stamps, etc.

- Will you have someone coming in
  to clean the house? Or do you

need to rent chairs, etc.?

- After you have the master budget, add about 10% more because there are always unexpected expenses that crop up. If that brings the amount up too high, then you can go back over the costs that you have allocated to the previous items.

- Have potluck meals and Secret Santa gift giving to keep your costs down.

- You can decide not to do what you always do and don't send cards, which you can save on the cards and stamps. Only send cards to people you will not see during the holidays.

- Keep your holiday receipts all in one place…online or offline shopping. Also, include the liquor and food shopping receipts.   This way you know if you stayed within your budget.   A box or a file in your file cabinet works great to keep them all in one place.

- I've added a "Holiday Budget List" at the end to help you.

Gift Buying on a Budget

- Give a gift of time of babysitting, making dinner, fix something for them, drive them somewhere.

- For large families, have a "Secret Santa" or "Hanukkah Hush Hush" for the extended family…you buy one gift for one person. Put a cap on how much you should spend.

- Only buy for the children and bring over some "goodies" for the adults to enjoy.

- Share with others your cooking talent. Create packages of cookies or a special bread that you made.
- Picture frame – with a picture of the family.

Unexpected Guests

It's always a good idea to keep some generic gifts on hand…for the unexpected guest who decides to give you a gift. I know it is not mandatory to give back a gift, yet you may prefer to have something ready to share with them. Here are some excellent gift ideas:

- Gift card to a local store or online store
- Bottle of wine or liquor
- Coffee or tea basket
- Candles
- Candy
- Nuts in a pretty container
- Movie tickets – if they are local guests

- Inexpensive, though a tasteful picture frame.

Keep on hand, small gifts that you and your family can use for yourself or for another occasion where a gift is necessary. Wrap up the gift and put a sticky on the bottom, so you know what is in it. Then you can graciously give a return gift to the person.

TRAVEL PLANS

Planning

If your holidays include traveling, here are some tips to make the journey easier.

By Plane
- Get plenty of sleep the night before

because traveling by plane takes a lot of energy and you want to be rested to handle the travel day.

- Try to schedule your travel dates a little earlier than the major travel day or come back a day later. You may be able to reduce costs, and your flexibility will lessen the travel stress. When you are searching for dates to travel, there is usually a choice "flexible travel dates." See if it works for you.

- Plan your shopping for the best time and fare ahead of time. This way you have time to comparison shop.

- When traveling during the peak holiday season, leave early because there can be traffic jams and long security check-in lines.

- Read the TSA rules before traveling, so you are not delayed in the security check-in line.

- It seems that the best time to travel is either early in the day or late in the day. Most people prefer the comfort of regular hours, so are willing to board during the busiest times of the day.

- If you are using frequent flyer options, investigate your best

options because miles can be
blocked out during peak holiday
times.

- Holiday times are known for delays
so make sure you call ahead to
check your flight time.

- If you are traveling by plane, you
can't wrap your presents ahead of
time. Security will make you
unwrap them. Instead, either bring
wrapping paper with you or wrap
them in a pretty bag that can also
serve as a gift. Even better, shop
online and send the packages in
your name, in the care of another
amily member.   If you are

traveling internationally, then buy
on Amazon, though in the country
you are visiting, so you don't pay
lots of shipping charges.

- Going through Security line, the
  left side seems to have fewer
  people because most people turn
  towards the right. All those years
  of staying in the right lane either on
  the road or going through a door
  have trained most people to lean
  right.

- Bring an empty water bottle, and
  after you go through Security, you
  can fill it up.

By Car

The trip could potentially be more extended, though that depends on how far you are going.

- Before you start your travel, have your car checked to make sure all the standard functions of the vehicle are in good shape.

- Plan your route and have roadside information on hand in case you need help. Check the weather.

- Keep all your valuable stuff in the trunk.

- Keep an emergency kit in the car: sand or cat litter, shovel, gloves &

blankets, flashlights, rags, drinking water and food in case you have a long wait.

- Start your travel either early or later at night because lots of people are traveling during the holidays and this is an excellent way to beat the traffic.

- Bring food and stop at a local rest area and eat your snack or meal. Have healthy snacks available throughout the trip, especially for young children. You can pack one special, not entirely healthy snack, they love.

- Plan to take lots of breaks, and it's good for your body as well as your level of driving concentration. I know lots of people think that speed when traveling is the most essential and stopping feels like a waste of time. When you slow down, your focus is on enjoying the holidays and little more time to get someplace only means you were able to see more during the journey.

- The recommendation is you take a break every two hours or 100 miles.

- Drivers can get frustrated when

traveling during the holidays. Keep
an eye out for aggressive drivers
and be safe by not responding to
them and letting them pass.

- If you can travel on the holiday
  itself, early in the day, it may be
  less stressful.

- If you get tired while driving, pull
  off the road. Nothing is worth your
  life.

- Bring music, audio books and
  whatever makes the drive
  comfortable for you. I bring them
  both, along with my lollipops
  (enjoyable sugar to increase my

energy.)

Traveling with Children

It depends on the age of the child, on how much planning you need to do to make the trip enjoyable for everyone.

- Toddlers may sleep through some of the trip, though most will need to be entertained. Bring books, movies, and games. Bring plenty of snacks.

- By plane, get up with them for a walk in the plane. Unless the child is noisy, most people like seeing a cute kid.

- When traveling by car, I use to play

who can find the most state license plates, or I Spy games. Today's kids have movies they can watch and music they can listen to. My grandchildren (ages 3 and 6) watched Netflix on their iPad, and that entertains them for a while.

- Plan a special holiday music tape that everyone can sing along with during the trip.

- I read on "Travel Mamas" website several good ideas and this is one of them: Kids can earn money by 1) who is the quietest during a period in the car, 2) who sleeps during the trip, 3) who plays nicely

with the other kids, and you can
think of your ideas. Then when
you stop somewhere, they can use
the money to buy something. I
know it sounds like bribery, but it's
for a good cause, and that is a
happy journey for all.

- Another idea is to create a unique
  travel bag for each of them, only to
  be opened on their trip. This is
  good for a plane or car travel.

- Do you own research to find ideas
  for traveling with children that fit
  your family.

Traveling with Pets

You may decide to find a good

babysitting arrangement at home for your pet or take them with you. If I'm not going with my family, I'm the designated babysitter for the cat, and he is great to watch.

If you decide to take your pet, here are some travel ideas to make is less stressful:

- Depending on how you are traveling, check to see what the policy is for the airline or train you are using during the holidays. You also have to check the hotels to see what their policy is around holidays.

- Research airline and airport security policies. TSA and your airline may have different policies around your pet. The policy will be based on the specific animal, weight and the season you are traveling.

- Some airlines require a vet certificate that they have clearance over a specific period.

- If your pet has a comfort toy, bring it with you.

- Make sure your pet has an identification tag, with your cell phone number. Many people put a microchip on their pet with the vital information.

- Each airline has different requirements for carriers for each animal, so again check with them. Many types of carriers/crates support the wellbeing of the animal.

- If you are traveling in a car, it may be good to put them in a crate in the back of the car or get a special harness that keeps them from jumping all over the car.

- I read recently to bring everything your animal is used to, and this ensures the experience is comfortable. Also mentioned is that cats especially can be fussy about their kitty litter, so bring their box and litter. Bring their food and any familiar bedding. Of course, if they are on medication, bring it as well.

- Try to keep your animal on a regular schedule by feeding them or taking them for a walk at regular times.
- Do your research, so you are providing your pet with the best experience.

Miscellaneous Travel Tips

- When I pack a bag, I put dryer sheets throughout the bag to keep clothes fresh.

- When you are packing liquids, you will need a clear quart Ziploc bag, so airport security can quickly view the contents. This is also good in case a bottle opens during a flight, and it won't damage your clothes.
- Reminder again, check out TSA rules to make sure you don't pack what is not acceptable, as well as the correct sizes of liquids for your flight.

- Remember to smile because that lightens the stress of traveling. When someone opens the door for you, thank them with a smile. If someone is helping you with your luggage, you will probably tip them, but also give them a big thanks for making your life easier. Wish people a "Happy Holidays." You will feel much lighter.

- When I travel, I print my name and number, as well as the hotel information, and tuck it on top of my suitcase, in case my bag is misplaced.

- Don't overpack. Most places can get clothes cleaned. If you are staying with family or friends, they have washing machines. I had to pack a small suitcase for a 12-day Scotland trip. I brought clothes that could be rinsed out, and I layered clothes to keep warm, and I managed to have a great time. Along the way at a Bed & Breakfast, for a small price, I got my dirty clothes cleaned.

- Most places you stay at will have shampoo, soap and hair dryers, so you don't need to pack them. Check with the hotel before you leave.

- Give your phone a full charge.

- Download your airline's app, so it keeps you informed of any changes.

PLANNING TOOLS

I've added some simple, ready to use tools (see below) to help you be more organized during the holidays. Use the samples to create your own and make as many copies as you need. What is your most important tool:

Planning

Save your completed lists for next year. You will know what you brought each person the previous year. When the new next holiday season comes around again, you are more prepared. Before you put the list away, make some notes on the back of the appropriate sheets on what worked or didn't work, and what would you do differently next year.

Create Your "To Do" lists:

Holiday Master List

- Use this list to put everything you need to do for the holidays. For example, gift shopping, menu planning, decorations organized, invites sent out for any parties you are planning, clothes shopping, travel arrangements…whatever else needs to be done for the holidays.

- Put the name of the person who is responsible for the activity.
- Put the date for completion next to it.

- If you are in charge of the Master List, you will probably need to put on your TO DO list a reminder to the others of their completion date.

- Don't forget to include organizing the decorations ahead of time. Missing lights and hangers for the tree decorations can be so frustrating when you need them the most.

- What about organizing and cleaning the house…important to delegate this chore. Either use family members to help or buy time from an outside cleaning company to help you. If you go outside, then don't forget to add the cost into your holiday budget.

Holiday Master Budget List

- Add all possible holiday expenses: gifts, food, drinks, travel, cleaning, wrapping, etc.

Holiday Gift List

- List all the people you want to give a gift.

- Create some gift ideas for each person. This is a perfect activity to do over a cup of coffee or tea...a time when you are relaxed. Your creativity flows better when you slow down to enjoy this activity. Build in some time to make some calls to others to get ideas. Once you have a master gift list, your shopping will be more efficient and productive…more fun.

- Start your shopping as early as possible.

- Put dates down on the list when you plan on shopping for the gifts and keep your calendar in front of you to plan the time. You can use the time to go to the stores or buy online, but you have scheduled the time to buy for people on your list.

When you are done, you can have the satisfaction of checking off their names on the list.

- Don't forget to include your budget for each of them. In the budget include tax, shipping and wrapping. You have to pay for it all.

- Use the back of the list to capture any notes you may want to keep.

Holiday Party Planning

- What is the theme of the party
- How many people will be invited

- When to send out the invites

- Plan time to create the menu

- Do you need extra chairs?

- Check your paper goods inventory before you go out shopping. If you traditionally have a holiday party…you may have extras left over from last year. The list can be extensive depending on how big of a gathering you are having.

- Always put a date next to the activity and put it on your calendar.

Holiday Planning Menu

- Make a list of everything you want to serve during the day: appetizers, drinks, main dishes, vegetables, bread, etc.

- Check your wine and liquor inventory to see what you need.

- Don't forget the ice or ask a dependable person to bring it.

- If you are having a potluck gathering, put each person's name next to it.

- In the section "by when" put in the date and time. On the day of the gathering, I schedule the exact times I will be preparing, cooking, etc.

- When do you put the item in to the oven? If you are cooking several different dishes, they may need different times and temperatures…it's all about organizing.

Holiday Food Shopping List

- Make a few copies of this List

- Create a list of every food or drink item you need. Review your recipes.

- After completing the list, now it's time to take an inventory of what you have already.

- Then create a new list of the actual items you need to go shopping.

HOLIDAY LIST FORMS

Holiday Master "To Do" List

Use to complete each task that needs to be completed and the list may be extensive:

Action to Be Completed	Who Does It	When

Holiday Master "Budget" List

List what you want to spend during the holidays so that you can control expenses.

Expense	Estimated Amount	Actual Amount
Gifts:		
Food:		
Drinks		
Travel		

TOTAL ESTIMATED

AMOUNT: _____

Holiday Gift List

Fill in each person you need to purchase a gift. Don't forget you can also delegate shopping to others.

Person	Gift Idea	Amount Budgeted	By When

Holiday Party Planning

This is a great tool to list all the action steps for the gathering.

Action to Be Completed	Who Does It	By When

Holiday Menu Planning

Use to complete each task that needs to be completed for:

Food Choices	Who Does It	When

Holiday Food Shopping List

Use to complete each task that needs to be completed for:

What You Need to Buy	What Store	When

Summary

Having a fantastic, enjoyable, less stressful holiday season can be done by using the tips suggested here. In any case, I hope that you have the best, most memorable holiday season ever, however you celebrate it, and with whomever, is part of your celebration.

About the Author

Pat Brill has spent many years planning family gatherings: Trim the Tree party, Open House party (over 30 years,) Hanukkah Hush Hush, engagement celebration and many small gatherings for family and friends. She loves researching different themes and ways to celebrate a special occasion and keeping it simple. Her focus is to create an environment where everyone can be themselves and enjoy each other.

Besides celebration planning, she also like to provide solutions to problems people face daily in their lives. She has created the following guides that help people deal with a specific situation that they need to address.

- How to Deal with a Compulsive Talker

- Procrastination Solutions Series: Stop Procrastinating and Find Your Next Job

- Managing Employees Series: Recruiting the Best Talent

- Managing Employees Series: Performance Management: Is It Time to Coach, Counsel or Terminate

- Managing Employees Series: How to Manage Your Time: To Get the Best Results

She has an extensive Human Resources background and knows the issues that managers face each day as they manage their teams.

Future guides will deal with more procrastination issues, women, and senior topics. She loves learning and researching for practical tips to make life easier and more enjoyable and sharing it with others.

If you have any great holiday tip ideas, you can reach her at pat@theinfocrowd.com

www.ingramcontent.com/pod-product-compliance
Lightning Source LLC
Chambersburg PA
CBHW062005040426
42447CB00010B/1923